My Family and Me

Poems about People

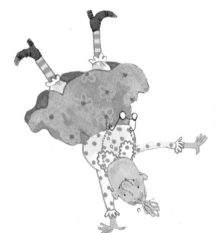

Chosen by John Foster

OXFORD

OXFORD

UNIVERSITY PRESS

Great Clarendon Street, Oxford OX2 6DP

Oxford University Press is a department of the University of Oxford.
It furthers the University's objective of excellence in research, scholarship,
and education by publishing worldwide in

Oxford New York

Athens Auckland Bangkok Bogotá Buenos Aires
Cape Town Chennai Dar es Salaam Delhi Florence Hong Kong Istanbul
Karachi Kolkata Kuala Lumpur Madrid Melbourne Mexico City Mumbai
Nairobi Paris São Paulo Shanghai Singapore Taipei Tokyo Toronto
Warsaw

with associated companies in Berlin Ibadan

Oxford is a registered trade mark of Oxford University Press
in the UK and in certain other countries

We are grateful to the authors for permission to reprint the following poems.

First published in John Foster (ed.): *Beep Goes My Belly-Button* (OUP, 1999):
Sue Cowling: 'Toenails', © Sue Cowling 1999; **Babs Bell Hajdusiewicz**: 'I
Like Me', © Babs Bell Hajdusiewicz 1999; **Tony Langham**: 'Beep Goes My
Belly-Button', © Tony Langham 1999; **Judith Nicholls**: 'Who's Scared?',
© Judith Nicholls 1999; **Jack Ousbey**: 'Feet', © Jack Ousbey 1999; **Paul
Rogers**: 'My Brother Says', © Paul Rogers 1999; **Celia Warren**: 'All Brand
New', © Celia Warren 1999.

First published in John Foster (ed.): *This is the Mum* (OUP, 1999):
Andrew Collett: 'My Dad Sleeps in the Rabbit Hutch' and 'Grandad
Remembered', both © Andrew Collett 1999; **Wes Magee**: 'Gran's Old Diary',
© Wes Magee 1999; **Paul Rogers**: 'Yuck', © Paul Rogers 1999; **Roger
Stevens**: 'My Family and Me', © Roger Stevens 1999.

We are also grateful for permission to reprint the following poems:
Tony Bradman: 'This is the Mum' from *All Together Now* (Viking Kestrel,
1987), © Tony Bradman 1987, reprinted by permission of The Agency
(London) Ltd. All rights reserved and enquiries to The Agency, 24 Pottery
Lane, London W11 4LZ; **John Cunliffe**: 'A Face in the Glass' from *There's A
Dinosaur in the Garden*, reprinted by permission of David Higham Associates;
Eleanor Farjeon: 'Bedtime' from *Something I Remember* (Puffin), reprinted by
permission of David Higham Associates. **John Foster**: 'Night-time, Fright-
time', from *You Little Monkey* (OUP, 1996), © John Foster 1996, reprinted by
permission of the author; **Margaret Hillert**: 'Hide-and-Seek Shadow' from
Farther Than Far (Follett Publishing, 1969), reprinted by permission of the
author who controls all rights; **Pamela Mordecai**: 'Remember' first
published in *Story Poems: A First Collection* (Ginn), reprinted by permission of
the author; **Spike Milligan**: 'My Sister Laura' from *Silly Verse for Kids* (Puffin,
1968), reprinted by permission of Spike Milligan Productions Ltd;
A. A. Milne: 'The End' from *Now We Are Six* (Methuen, an imprint of Egmont
Children's Books Ltd, London, and Dutton Children's Books, an imprint of
Penguin Putnam Books for Young Readers, a division of Penguin Putnam,
Inc), copyright 1927 by E. P. Dutton, renewed © A. A. Milne 1955 under the
Berne Convention, reprinted by permission of the publishers; **Brian Patten**:
'Squeezes' from *Gargling with Jelly* (Viking, 1985), copyright © Brian Patten
1985, reprinted by permission of Penguin Books Ltd, and the author, c/o
Rogers, Coleridge & White Ltd, 20 Powis Mews, London W11 1JN; **Jack
Prelutsky**: 'Somersaults' from *Rainy Day Saturday* (Greenwillow Books),
copyright © 1980 by Jack Prelutsky reprinted by permission of HarperCollins
Publishers, New York, and 'My Baby Brother' from *The New Kid on the Block*,
(Greenwillow Books, and Heinemann Young Books, an imprint of Egmont
Children's Books Ltd), copyright © 1984 by Jack Prelutsky, reprinted by
permission of HarperCollins Publishers, New York, and Egmont Children's
Books Ltd; **Asma Tabassum**: 'Eid' first published in Jennifer Curry (ed.):
Them and Us (Bodley Head, Red Fox 1993), reprinted by permission of The
Random House Group Ltd.

Despite efforts to obtain permission from all copyright holders before
publication, this has not been possible in a few cases. If notified the
publisher will be pleased to rectify any errors or omissions at the earliest
opportunity.

The illustrations are by:
Ivan Bates p. 32; Emma Dodd pp. 4–5, 26; Adriano Gon pp. 11, 16, 28–29;
Rebecca Gryspeerdt pp. 12–13;
Charlotte Hard pp. 22–23; Rhian Nest James pp. 6–7, 30–31; Tessa
Richardson Jones pp. 14–15; Jan McCafferty pp. 10, 24;
Ken Wilson Max p. 17; Martin Shovel p. 25; Caroline Uff pp. 18–19, 20–21;
Woody pp. 8–9, 27

List of contents:

I Like Me!

This morning I stood up and said:

I like myself from toes to head!
I like the way I look today!
I like the way I work and play!

4

I like the way I act with friends!
I like the way my body bends!
I like who I was born to be!
I like myself!
  Hey!
    I like ME!

Babs Bell Hajdusiewicz

This is the Mum

This is the mum
Who wakes me up
And gets me out of bed.

This is the mum
Who helps me pull
My clean vest over my head.

This is the mum
Who irons my clothes
Who puts out my clean socks.

This is the mum
Who puts my lunch
Inside my new lunchbox.

This is the mum
Who goes to work
Who tries not to be late.

This is the mum
Who stands in the rain
By the infant gate.

Tony Bradman

Remember

Remember when
the world was tall
and you were small
and legs were all you saw?

Thin legs
Fat legs
Dog legs
Cat legs

Dark legs
Fair legs
Table legs
Chair legs

Quick legs
Slow legs

Nowhere-to-go legs

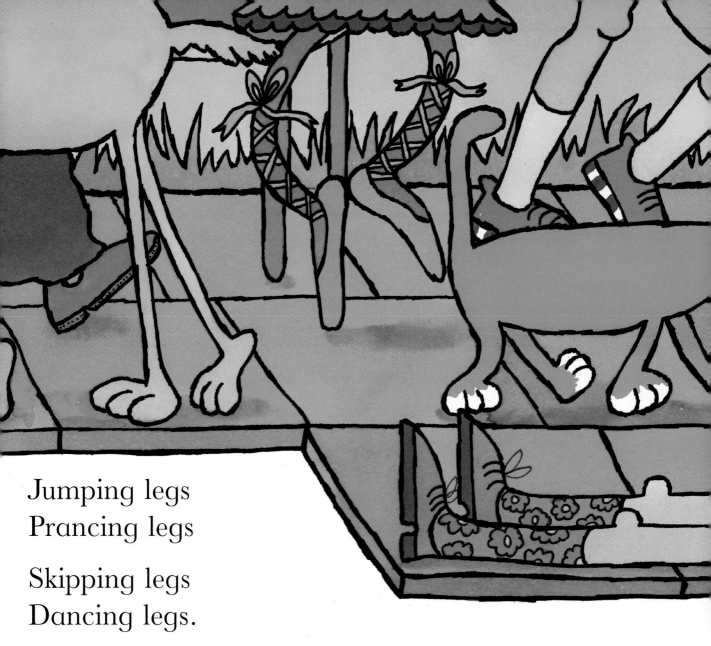

Jumping legs
Prancing legs

Skipping legs
Dancing legs.

Shoes-and-sock legs
On-the-rocks legs.

Standing-very-tall legs
Running-all-around legs

Stooping-very-small legs
Lying-on-the-ground legs.

Remember when
the world was tall
and you were small
and legs were all you saw?

Pamela Mordecai

My Family and Me

Dad is like a hippo
with a great big yawn
Mum is like a lion
stretched out on the lawn
My sister's like a monkey
hanging from a tree,
But I am like a wise old owl
as brainy as can be.

Roger Stevens

A Face in the Glass

One, two, three,
I can see,
A face in the glass
looking at me;
Is it mine,
Or is it another?
Looking-glass sister,
Looking-glass brother?
It copies all
the things I do,
Purses its lips
When I say "Boo!"
But it lives in a place
Inside the glass
Where I can never
ever pass.
Looking-glass sister,
Looking-glass brother?
Is it me
or is it another?

John Cunliffe

Eid

The moon is rising
Ramadan's ended
Eid is here – Hooray!

Mums are cooking
Men are praying
Girls henna their hands – Hooray!

Families are gathering
With presents and money
Mum brings us all food – Hooray!

Asma Tabassum
(12 years)

13

Gran's Old Diary

I found my Gran's old diary.
  It has a lock and key.
I found it in the attic
  when mum explored with me.

My Gran wrote her old diary
  many years ago.
She used the blackest ink
  on pages white as snow.

And inside Gran's old diary
  something caught my eye.
It was a tiny buttercup
  pressed flat from years gone by.

Wes Magee

Me and Elsie
Torquay

23rd May
Mummy and Dad
took me to whiteway
woods for a picnic. We

Grandad Remembered

The best thing in our house
the best thing of all,
is the old armchair
sat alone in the hall.

It's tattered and torn
it's dirty and brown,
its stuffing comes out
when you try to sit down.

But it's still the best thing
the best thing of all,
for that's where my grandad
used to sit in the hall.

Andrew Collett

Hide-and-Seek Shadow

I walked with my shadow,
I ran with my shadow,
I danced with my shadow,
I did.
Then a cloud came over
And the sun went under
And my shadow stopped playing
And hid.

Margaret Hillert

Squeezes

We love to squeeze bananas.
We love to squeeze ripe plums.
And when they are feeling sad,
We love to squeeze our mums.

Brian Patten

Beep Goes My Belly-Button

Beep goes
my belly-button,

Honk goes
my nose.

Click, clack
go my teeth,

Jingle, jangle
go my toes.

Tony Langham

Toenails

These are the nails
That guard the toes
That fit the foot
That wore the boot
That kicked the ball
That scored the goal
That won the match
On Sunday!

Sue Cowling

My Brother Says

We're full of bones, my brother says,
Inside this bag of skin.
We'd rattle if it weren't for all
Those squidgy bits stuffed in.

But even worse, my brother says,
(I'll get this over quick)
All our lives we walk around
With tummies full of sick!

Paul Rogers

My Baby Brother

My baby brother is so small,
he hasn't even learned to crawl.
He's only been around a week,
and all he seems to do is bawl
and wiggle, sleep... and leak.

Jack Prelutsky

My Little Sister

My little sister
Likes to eat.
But when she does
She's not too neat.
The trouble is
She doesn't know
Exactly where
The food should go.

William Wise

Yuck

Jam all over her fingers,
Pastry in her hair,
Fruit juice dribbling down her chin
And custard *every*where.

Playdough in her fingernails,
Mud between her toes,
And something much much nastier
Running from her nose.

But none of that would bother me
If it weren't for this:
My sister's heading this way fast –
And it's *me* she wants to kiss!

Paul Rogers

Somersaults

It's fun turning somersaults
and bouncing on the bed,
I walk on my hands
and I stand on my head.

I swing like a monkey
and I tumble and I shake,
I stretch and I bend,
but I never, never break.

I wiggle like a worm
and I wriggle like an eel,
I hop like a rabbit
and I flop like a seal.

I leap like a frog
and I jump like a flea,
there must be a rubber
inside of me.

Jack Prelutsky

My Sister Laura

My sister Laura's bigger than me
And lifts me up quite easily.
I can't lift her, I've tried and tried;
She must have something heavy inside.

Spike Milligan

My Dad Sleeps in the Rabbit Hutch

My dad sleeps in our rabbit hutch
because of his terrible snore,
Mum feeds him every morning
with toast and bits of straw.

Andrew Collett

All Brand New

Come and see my bedroom.
It's all brand new.
The walls were pink before
but they're now sky blue.

I've got a fluffy carpet,
and a shiny yellow shelf,
and a blue and yellow picture
that I painted myself.

But the best thing of all
is my big bunk bed.
I'm as happy as can be
that my bed is RED!

Celia Warren

Feet

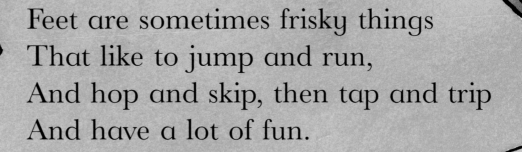

Feet are very useful things,
They often come in twos,
They like to make their home in socks
Or wellybobs or shoes.

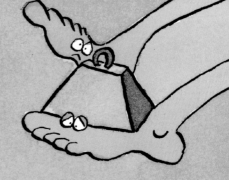

Feet are sometimes frisky things
That like to jump and run,
And hop and skip, then tap and trip
And have a lot of fun.

Feet are sometimes tired out
And feel like weights of lead,
And the only spot they like a lot
Is the bottom of the bed.

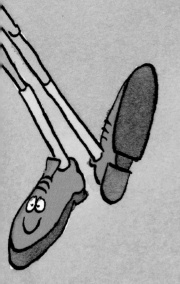

So close your eyes and settle down
Underneath the sheet,
Then whisper goodnight to everyone,
Especially your feet.

Jack Ousbey

Who's Scared?

It's late, it's dark,
I'm still awake,
but am I scared?

Not me!

A window bangs,
the cold wind howls,
but I'm not scared.

Not me!

A door slams shut,
a night owl hoots,
I hear a loud

Wheee-heee!

I hear a step
outside my door,
but who is scared?

Not...

ME!

Judith Nicholls

Night-time, Fright time

Night-time, fright time,
Please leave on the light time.

Night-time. Shadows creep.
Floorboards creak. Can't sleep.

Night-time, fright time,
Please leave on the light time.

Night-time. Darkness hides.
Goblin chuckles. Ghost glides.

Night-time, fright time,
Please leave on the light time.

Night-time, fear time,
Something's creeping near time.

Night-time, fright time,
PLEASE LEAVE ON THE LIGHT TIME!

John Foster

Bedtime

Five minutes, five minutes more, please!
　Let me stay five minutes more!
Can't I just finish the castle
　I'm building here on the floor?
Can't I just finish the story
　I'm reading here in my book?
Can't I just finish this bead-chain –
　It's *almost* finished, look!
Can't I just finish this game, please?
　When a game's once begun
It's a pity never to find out
　Whether you've lost or won.
Can't I stay five minutes?
　Well, can't I stay just four?
Three minutes, then? two minutes?
　Can't I stay *one* minute more?

Eleanor Farjeon

The End

When I was One
I had just begun.

When I was Two
I was nearly new.

When I was Three
I was hardly Me.

When I was Four
I was not much more.

When I was Five
I was just alive.

But now I am Six, I'm as clever as clever.
So I think I'll be six now for ever and ever.

A.A. Milne